Written in the Stars

An Anthology

Edited by Sabrina Favors

Savant Books and Publications
Honolulu, HI, USA
2015

Published in the USA by Savant Books and Publications LLC
2630 Kapiolani Blvd #1601
Honolulu, HI 96826
http://www.savantbooksandpublications.com

Printed in the USA

Edited by Sabrina Favors
Cover by Daniel S. Janik
Cover and Interior Images Copyright 2014 by Na Hokulele Project.

13 digit ISBN: 978-0-9915622-5-1

This book is primarily non-fictional in nature, with stories and personal accounts collected from various cultural sources. The publisher has endeavored to ensure accuracy; however, due to the collection of accounts through written and oral sources, there may remain both typographical and content errors.

The work that provided the basis for this publication was supported by funding under Grant Number AHIAC-10-HI-01 with the U.S. Department of Housing and Urban Development, Office of University Partnerships. The authors and publisher are solely responsible for the accuracy of the statements and interpretations contained in this publication. Such interpretations do not necessarily reflect the views of the Government.

Dedication

This anthology is dedicated to Sherone Ivey, the HUD Deputy Assistant Secretary, Office of University Partnerships, and Ramona Mullahey, the HUD Senior Analyst, Field Policy and Management, for their heartfelt commitment to the success of Na Hokulele participants. A special dedication goes to the women, men, youth and children who have opened up their lives and shared their stories with readers.

Acknowledgements

Our sincerest aloha to Hawai'i Pacific University; Krause Family Foundation: 'Alana Ke Aloha; St. Elizabeth's Episcopal Church; Ala Moana Barnes & Noble Booksellers (formerly at Kahala Mall); Times Coffee Shop, Kailua; University of Hawai'i at Manoa, CTAHR, Magoon Research Station; Honolulu Museum of Art; St. Damien Memorial School; Heald College Honolulu; Savant Books and Publications; and Honolulu Community Action Program (HCAP). The Na Hokulele Project (NHP) and *Written in the Stars: An Anthology* were developed and will be sustained thanks to the generous help and support of dedicated, community partners.

Thank you to the teachers, staff and mentors of the Na Hokulele Project, along with those faculty at St. Damien Memorial School and the Honolulu Museum of Art School who shared their experience and enthusiasm. Special thanks also goes to Juliette Budge with whom NHP participants talked story and shared dozens of their experiences. She was invaluable in the creation of this anthology. Finally, every writer needs an editor. Our heartfelt gratitude to Sabrina Favors whose reverent editing brought *Written in the Stars: An Anthology* to life.

"Even through your hardest days, remember we are all made of stardust."

- Carl Sagan

Table of Contents

Written in the Stars

List of Authors

One of the central values in Pacific Island culture is the importance and emphasis of the community over the individual. To highlight an individual's story with their name beside it could cause feelings of discomfort for many contributors. Because many of our authors come from Pacific Islander backgrounds, we have opted to list all of their names together, alphabetically, below. Only a few select stories, at the authors' request, include their name beside their story.

Marciano Aliwis	Joshua Lino
Kathy Andereas	P.K. Miecho
Pious Casiano (Father)	K.O. Muludy
Pious Casiano (Son)	Kimbo Nick
Inoleen Eichy	T-Boy Nuokus
Eniko Esefan	Cecilia Pita
Kevin Espin	Debra Puailoa
Brenson Felix	Kristina Sipenuk
Fr. David Gierlach	Shellie Ann Steffey
Tony Gilbert	Ignacia Terno
Sepestiana Joseph	Tim Terno
Fabian Kosnes	Starlyte Yockman

All artwork has been provided by Na Hokulele youth participants.

Emergent Literacy

Preface: Rewriting Destiny

They say destiny is written in the stars. What will be is set in stone. You can't change the past. For those living in poverty, newly arrived from another state or country, or dealing with trauma and challenges, a past full of hardship can make the future seem bleak. A never-ending struggle.

Despite disadvantages from all sides, the storytellers in this anthology see a different future for themselves, their families and communities. They are striving to take the lessons of the past, together with new skills, to create a destiny full of promise and hope. Perhaps, if destiny *is* written in the stars, then these stars *can* rewrite destiny.

Introduction: From Shooting Stars to Writing Stars

Written in the Stars is an anthology of stories, "news" and poems written by participants of the Na Hokulele ("Shooting Stars") Project (NHP), a grant funded by the HUD Office of University Partnerships, Alaska Native/Native Hawaiian Institutions Assisting Communities (AN/NHIAC) Program (2011-2015) with Hawai'i Pacific University (HPU), Krause Family Foundation, 'Alana Ke Aloha (KFF) and key community partners. The participants are community residents of a low-income community in Honolulu, Hawai'i, and include children, youth and adults who attend the NHP afterschool and Saturday programs as well as freshmen from the Success100 course at the nearby Heald College, Honolulu Campus.

NHP's primary goal is to increase the participants' and community's interest in, and knowledge about, literacy, STEM, higher education and related job readiness and training opportunities.

In a perfect universe, a grant project's formal objectives and the ever-changing needs of participants and their community remain aligned. Although few things are perfect, NHP strives to keep that alignment. The project often resembles a two-dimensional rendering of a constellation: dot after dot after dot connects the stars in an effort to understand and give shape to the nascent.

We do our star work "in community," teaching and learning *through* our participants' cultures. In our tremendously diverse city of Honolulu, this is defined as (a) teachers with deep respect for and knowledge of our families' languages, cultures and socio-economic structures; (b) an unconditional belief in our children, youth and adults, which we communicate regularly to our participants; (c) relevant learning activities that challenge racial, ethnic and socio-economic stereotypes; (d) a caring, learning environment that extends beyond the immediate project site, family home and neighborhood; (e) culturally sensitive instructional delivery such as flexible groupings and cooperative learning; and (f) culturally and linguistically responsive assessment such as work samples, teacher observations, anecdotes and rubrics.

Written in the Stars: An Anthology provides students an opportunity to share, from their perspective, what it is like to be on the receiving end of a grant project like NHP, and for some, what it is like in the next stage, as newly enrolled college students. As the grantee, we have evaluative data to tell us what "success" looks like and are confident that our participants are achieving success as we've defined it. However, our data do not, and cannot, tell us what participant success *feels* like.

We believe it is important to acknowledge the many ways our participants feel along the road to success. I am honored that our students have gifted us (and you, the reader) with their profound and intimate replies in the form of stories, "news," poetry, and, in some cases, skirting the language barrier, illustrations.

May the stars guide us.

- Suzanne Langford, PhD
Project Director
Na Hokulele Project
President
Krause Family Foundation: 'Alana Ke Aloha

The Strength and Influence of Family and Culture

"You don't choose your family.

They are God's gift to you, as you are to them."

- Desmond Tutu

Five Brothers and the Crocodile
Adult storyteller from Faichuuk

Nesor anim (good morning). This is a story about five brothers on the island of Paata. You might know them, they are named after your fingers: *Outunap* (thumb), *Outitit* (pointer), *Outunuk* (middle finger), *Outsapak* (ring finger) and *Outingin* (pinkie).

On the island of Paata, there is a large and hungry animal, a crocodile. The crocodile would eat the food and the people of Paata, so the five brothers were the only people willing to live on Paata at that time. When they would go fishing, one of them would stay and prepare *mai* (breadfruit) in the *um* (like an *imu*, an Hawaiian underground oven), so when the others would return home, they could enjoy a meal with the fish that they had caught that day.

One evening, when Outunap had stayed home to cook, and the *mai* was ready, the crocodile came to ask for food. Outunap gave everything to the animal because he was scared. The crocodile ate all the *mai*, so he was satisfied and he didn't eat the brother. When the other brothers got home from fishing, their arms were full of fish. Outunap told them that the crocodile had visited him, and had eaten all the *mai*, so that night for dinner, there was only fish.

The next night, Outitit stayed behind. That evening, just as the *mai* was becoming perfectly roasted, the crocodile slid into the kitchen, and again asked for food. Outitit was very afraid, and gave him all the *mai* he had cooked. When the other brothers returned home that night with fish, there was no *mai* because the crocodile had eaten it all, so they just ate fish.

The third day Outunuk stayed, and the fourth day Outsapak was to cook, and the crocodile visited and ate all the *mai* on both evenings. The next night, the fifth night, was Outingin's turn to stay home and cook while his brothers went fishing. But the brothers, they really loved their small brother, and were worried about letting him stay home alone, because they knew the crocodile would be coming. But Outingin, though small, was brave, and he said, "I can stay by myself and make our food so when you come home, we will eat *mai* and *ik* (fish)." So the other four brothers left to fish and Outingin prepared the *mai*.

Outingin did as the other brothers had, and made an *um*. When the stones had turned red with heat, the crocodile came. When the crocodile saw Outingin, he said, "You are so handsome, I want to be like you."

Outingin said, "Come. I will teach you how you can do that."

The crocodile wanted to be handsome like Outingin so he listened. Outingin said, "Come closer and open your mouth. I will take the red stone and put it in your mouth and your skin will change and become like mine." The crocodile came closer and opened his mouth and Outingin put the stones in his mouth, one by one.

When all the stones were in the mouth of the crocodile, his skin began to change, darkening to be just like Outingin's. And then the crocodile, having been cooked by the red rocks, died.

Soon after, the other brothers came home with arms full of fish. Outingin had already prepared some *kon* (pounded breadfruit) with water. They were so happy to see that Outingin was okay.

As they came near they said, "Oh, what are we going to eat?" thinking Outingin survived by giving the crocodile all the *mai*. But he said, "We have *kon* to eat with our fish."

"How can this be?" They asked if the crocodile had come and he said yes, it came. The brothers were amazed. "How come you can have this when the crocodile came? What did you do?"

He said, "There was something that the crocodile liked on me, so he wanted to be just like me. I said this is how you can be handsome like me. So I gave the crocodile the hot stones, and then the crocodile died."

The brothers relished how smart their small brother was, and they ate the *kon* with *ik*, and they were all happy.

The End

My sister told me this story—she is bigger than me—and the point is to learn that the small one in the family can do good things.

There is a tradition of story-telling that is passed on from grandparents to grandkids. We stay and they tell. When we stay with parents, they are too busy to tell us stories. And in Hawai'i, kids stay with their parents, not their grandparents, so aren't told as many stories. But stories are for passing on.

Together
Child storyteller from Chuuk

I liked the computers, I liked making videos
I remember Aunty Fane
She helped me with my homework.
I remember Ignacia, she would make us food.
My favorite was sausage.
My friends were there, too, like Anek.
He moved, I don't know where.
My brother came too, he is younger.
Eison liked coming.
It helped me become better at writing
And making pictures.

The Beach

Family Wisdom

Adult storyteller from Chuuk

All of the islands in Chuuk have magic, but the magic that they fear most is from the lagoon. It is known throughout the islands, whenever people come to Chuuk they have to be very careful because everything is kind of magical. They are afraid to come to Chuuk because Chuuk was known for strong magic.

Nemwes is seven feet tall, very tall, and she wanted to come to Chuuk to collect flowers. She liked the flowers in Chuuk, especially the *panaange*, because they are so beautiful and fragrant. We still have them today, and at night you can smell them; it is really beautiful.

Nemwes' father was the chief from Yap, and she needed his permission to go to Chuuk to collect the fragrant flowers. He finally gave in, but he warned her, "I want you to go and walk on the eastern side of the lagoon, not the northern side, that is where the strong magic is."

Nemwes also had magic and she put it on her feet so she could walk on water. It is a magic that only her family knows.

She set out and walked on the water for fifty or sixty miles. Finally, she reached the lagoon on the island of Udot. That is where all the flowers bloom, but that lagoon was also a dangerous place called

Fouchap. Nobody goes there without permission and without giving respect.

Her dad told her not to ever go to this place, never. But she wanted to go for the beautiful flowers, more beautiful because no one ever touches them. With her magic, she crossed the water, picked the flowers and hurried down from the mountain to go, but the people there saw her. They started to make their *um*, since at that time they didn't have pots and pans. At the bottom of the mountain, they asked her to eat. She wanted to eat, and already, she had not heeded her father's warnings—not to go there and especially not to eat or drink anything—so she sat down and started to eat breadfruit. She ate until she was full.

Nemwes got up and walked out to the beach, and as she stepped on the ocean, she sank into the water. She could no longer walk on the water. She tried to put the magic on her feet again, but just sank. She had to return to the beach and she started to cry and kick. When she realized she could not go back to her family, she made a ring of rocks around herself. She did that until she was exhausted and then she died there.

The people from the village buried her right where she lay.

Nemwes followed what she wanted instead of her family wisdom. She didn't heed her father's words.

Like My Dad
Pious Casiano (Son)

My name is Pious Casiano, and I am 10 years old. When I grow up I want to be a case worker because here, in my family, there are a lot of people who have problems, but when they speak up, they don't always find people that can help them. When I am a case worker, I will help people in need to get organized and if they have a problem, I will help them and tell them about the laws in America. Also, I would help the people that have a problem with their relatives and I would help the people who need to find a house. To do this, I need to keep going to school, listen and pay attention, and try my best in everything. My path ahead looks clear, because my dad now looks like a case worker; he helps lots of people.

The Legend of the Beginning, Kumulipo

Starlyte Yockman

Papa, the darkness

Wakea, the sky

From Papa and Wakea came Ho'ohokulani

From Wakea and Ho'ohokulani came the stillborn Haloanaka

Into the dirt went Haloanaka

From the dirt came the Kalo

From Wakea and Ho'ohokulani then came the second son Haloa

Haloa is to care for his elder brother Haloanaka

Haloanaka will in turn sustain his brother Haloa

This is our bond with the earth, sustainability, and the beginning of the
beginning

The genealogy of Hawaiians

Descendants of Haloa.

> *"Always leave a place better than you found it.*
> *That way you will always be able to come back."*
>
> -The Yockman and Kaukini Ohana

Uniforms

Adult storyteller from Chuuk

Women in Chuuk, it is our custom to wear dresses or skirts and blouses. Some we buy at the store and some we make; we sew them. We wear the skirts when we are at home, and when we are working, cooking, cleaning and washing. For gatherings and more formal things, we wear the *nikoutang* (the Chuukese version of a muumuu). It is really more special, and for important days.

A few months back, we got a chance to train to be home health care workers. We were really excited and maybe sixty or seventy of us signed up. Chuukese women, mothers and some teenagers, came to the training because they really want to get jobs. However, for the training, and to work as a home health caretaker, you needed to wear a uniform. This uniform has a blouse and *rausis* (long pants). That is the rule. When we are with other women, we are comfortable, and it doesn't matter whether we have pants on or skirts, but we do not want men to see us wear pants.

I would come to the training with pants in my bag and change there. Other women would wear a skirt over their pants. Once, a woman was wearing her uniform on the bus and a group of Chuukese women saw her, and they said, "Why are you wearing pants? Are you a nurse where you work?" She was surprised to see them and answered yes.

Some of the women are embarrassed to wear pants in front of their kids, but others said that their kids liked it, and thought it was cool. But you can imagine, it is an adjustment (since we never wear pants) to go to strangers' houses wearing the uniform. But we all do it, because we are looking for work, and need jobs, and these jobs pay much better than housekeeping or foodservice.

Never Leave Children Alone

Adult storyteller from Chuuk

There was a family who lived near the ocean. The Tumunun Family. The mother and father liked to fish together, and they had one son. When the son was old enough, they would go fishing at night after he went to bed. One night, the boy was alone and he heard an *onu sobe* (a type of ghost) call from on the ridge.

The ghost called down and said, "Are you alone?"

The boy was smart, so he said, "No, I am not alone, I have my uncles and aunties here, the neighbors from down the road and my cousins."

The ghost wanted to go down and eat him, but knew he could not if there were so many people around, so he left him alone.

The next day, the boy was worried about the ghost calling him again, so he went out into the forest and cut down banana stalks and hauled them back to his house. Inside, he stood the banana stalks up so they would look like people. That night, when his parents left him to go fishing, he heard the ghost call again. "Are you alone?"

"No, I am not alone, I have my friends here, and my grandparents, and the people from town that are visiting," the boy said.

This time, the ghost did not believe him, so he left the ridge of the mountain to check and see if what the boy said was true. When the ghost got to the house, he saw through the window all the silhouettes of people and knew he could not eat the boy with them there, so he went back to the ridge.

The next night, when the ghost called, and the boy answered, the ghost decided to check again. This time, he went to the door and peeked inside. He, of course, saw that these were not people, but banana stalks, so he rushed in and grabbed the boy. The boy began to scream for his parents, and luckily, they were just returning from their fishing trip. They ran to the house as the ghost ran away, back up the mountain.

The parents decided they would kill the ghost, so the father brought the huge pounding rock that they used to prepare breadfruit and he placed it over the doorway on a rafter. That night, instead of going fishing, the parents put the boy to bed and the father hid behind the gigantic stone and waited. When the ghost called, "Boy, are you alone?" the boy answered, "Why do you keep asking me that?" This aggravated the ghost, and sent him running down the hill from his ridge. When he got to the doorway, the father pushed the boulder onto him, and the ghost was smashed under the weight, his blood splattered on the ceiling.

The mother and father cleaned up the house, and collected all the parts of the ghost in a basket and dropped it into the deep sea.

The next night, the mother and father were so relieved that the ghost was gone, and that their son would be safe alone, that they left a little earlier to fish. The boy played for a while, and then got tired and went to bed. He hadn't been sleeping long when he heard the ghost's howl. The blood on the celling was calling to its body, and soon the parts had come from the sea and the ghost was whole again. The boy's parents were too far away to hear the boy cry for help, and he was eaten by the ghost.

The moral of the story is to never leave your kids alone, no matter how safe you think they are, you must always be near them to protect them when they are young.

Basic Needs Come Before Education

"…For neither life itself nor the good life is possible without a certain minimum supply of the necessities."

- Aristotle, *The Politics*, Book I

Hunger

It Matters

Youth storyteller from Chuuk

I was born in Chuuk in 2000.

I came to Hawai'i and I stayed for two years before moving back to Chuuk and stayed there until I moved back to Hawai'i in 2007.

I started school in 2008, 2nd grade at Kaiulani.

When I started school, it was scary. I had bullies at the school. One of them choked me and I told the teacher, and the bully told the teacher that I threw a rock at him, but he was lying. The teacher asked me if that was true and I nodded because I didn't know how to speak English. She scolded me.

I had to stay at the school, and in 3rd grade, the bully and I started to get along, and I became good friends with him. In elementary, I kind of did badly in school, but they still passed me, and I started doing better in 4th grade. There was a mean teacher in 4th grade, and she yelled and slammed the door, but I got along with her. She started saying, "You are doing good" and it made me feel good. I passed with better grades. Then in 5th grade, the teacher moved up, so I had her again, and when she retired that year, another teacher that was really nice came, and we got along. That year I graduated with even better grades. I would go visit my teacher after 5th grade because

I missed her. In 6th grade, I went to Central Middle School, along with my classmates. It was different, we had to walk around to our classes, but it was fun. Some of my teachers were good, others…they didn't understand us. In 6th grade, I had bad grades and had to go to summer school for math. I finished.

My teacher made us food last year. We ate, and then we could concentrate on our work. I stayed in her class, and she would give me food. In 7th grade, I didn't pass math again; I didn't do my homework. I also didn't do well in social studies and science. I might have to repeat 7th grade. The first semester I didn't get good grades. I did better the 4th quarter, but I still didn't pass.

To be continued…

Although the continuation is not included in this anthology, the story is not done.

Reality

Adult storyteller from Faichuuk, Polle
(Translated with help from Jade)

Once upon a time, there was a woman, she moved to Hawai'i in April of 2012. (This is a story about myself here.) I lived with my daughter in Waipahu. I lived with my daughter in Kam 4 housing, the others lived with the relative of my daughter's husband.

This year we moved out of the apartment. We could not afford to pay the rent because only two of us that lived there had jobs. I applied for housing. I have two sons, 32 and 22; they also lived with relatives until March when my two sons and I rented an apartment on Date Street. In April, the owner told us that they were going to renovate the house and we had to move out, so we moved after only living there one month. I moved back to Kam 4 and my sons moved in with their father. All their stuff had to be stored in a storage locker.

It has been a problem that we don't live together. Since I moved here in 2012 and have applied for affordable housing, I have been waiting. In Chuuk, we all lived together and here, since my sons don't have wives, they only have me. For months at a time, my sons and I do not see each other. We only talk by phone because we are far apart. It is really hard.

Before, in 2013, I had SSI, but in 2014 it stopped. They sent a letter, but I couldn't understand what it said. Not having a house makes things…more complicated. I don't have any money for food, so I sell my dresses. It is not so easy to sell dresses but when someone gives me the material I can sew the dress. I charge twenty dollars for a *nikota*, which is a more traditional Chuukese dress. I am happy here, but it has been hard with the financial stress and having no housing.

Princess and Queen

Shellie Ann Steffey, from Illinois

One day, there was a beautiful princess and queen.

They set off on a journey to find a princess dress that doesn't fit them and to find a princess that has a dress that does fit her.

The Queen doesn't have a dress that fits her, and this one, the little one, *does* have a dress that fits her.

The Queen and princess. And the Queen doesn't have a dress that fits her and This one does have the princess. the little one, a dress that fits her.

This is a mean princess.

The mean princess tries to take away the nice princess' power. This is all the power.

This is the rainbow of the power that NEVER gets taken away.

This is a princess with one eye and it can't even see. But it wants to see.

The song: This princess doesn't want her power taken away!

The author, now seven, was five years old when she wrote this story.

Resilience

"Search for what is good and strong and beautiful in your society and elaborate from there. Push outward. Always create from what you already have. Then you will know what to do."

- Michel Foucault

The Mother, the Baby and the Lightning

Adult storyteller from the Federated States of Micronesia (FSM)

On the island of Piis Paneu in the FSM, Chuuk State, there was a mother with a baby. This was long before the German Rule over our islands, so long ago, no one remembers when it was. The mother was a good lady, but her baby was crying all the time, day and night. The mother tried to stop the child, but the baby never stopped.

One night, it was raining and windy, and the child was crying so the mom had to go walk him by the beach. The lightning was striking all around, and she was wet, and the child kept crying. She had a wish, that the lightning would come down and stop the baby from crying.

Suddenly, the lightning came down and turned them into stone.

Be careful for your wishes, because sometimes they come true.

Homeless

Adult storyteller from Kaka'ako Park, Hawai'i

I moved to Hawai'i from California to help my son recover from surgery for spina bifida. The doctors said it would take two years for him to make a full recovery. I have now lived here for the past two years and faced many challenges. Finding a house big enough for me and my children was really hard. Landlords demand so many things and do not like to have many people living in their homes, but I have six children, so we need a bigger space. I have also been working jobs that pay minimum wage, but that doesn't cover rent, so now my family is homeless. I don't want my kids to not have opportunities because I am poor. Youth programs are important, like afterschool programs that give extra instruction. They help fill the gap that our economic situation creates.

Trying Hard

Youth storyteller from Chuuk

Summer School
I'm a kid that goes to summer school
Because I don't do good in school.
Just to get my grades through.
In math, I am failing.
I am trying hard to pass.
I don't want to repeat this course
And re-live the past.

Starlyte's Adventure

Starlyte Yockman

I remember abandonment.

I remember the coolness of the rain as it dripped through the tarp.

I remember being so tired I didn't care that the drips were now drenching me.

Lying there, hair and clothes soaked to the bone, passed out.

Nights like those happened often.

Living homeless in Waimanalo, reminiscing about the past.

The struggles of my past are what shaped me into the person that I am. Homelessness was one of the hardships my family and I faced. Being homeless had its difficulties but my parents made sure we had all we needed, most of the time. I remember them carrying in large containers of water by hand to where we were camped. We always lived where people wouldn't see us because they would always call the police and my parents would be threatened with CPS taking us away.

Culturally, this life was normal for us and brought us that much closer to nature. The ocean was our front yard while the Ko'olau Mountains were our backyard.

My father would lay net to catch the fish while we (the keiki) would scale and gut them. We ate what we caught and shared with others also, as they did with us. Living with nature you become one with it. We were able to tell when a storm was coming in and from what direction. The direction it came from determined (usually) the type or even how bad the storm could be for us. The smell in the wind would tell us from what direction it was coming. If you've noticed when it gets humid and stale, something's holding the wind back; it's most likely a storm. When the wind begins to blow suddenly, you can tell the storm is breaking. The clouds are unloading. As it clears the way, it also releases oxygen, which is why the wind will gust unexpectedly.

A few of the downsides to being homeless were abandonment, molestation and rape. I have gone through all of them. My parents' addiction to partying and associating with others who also liked to party made them that much more blind to the possibilities that someone could hurt us in that way.

When we moved to town away from our Hawaiian way of life, we met new challenges but some of the same old problems. Drugs and alcohol somehow followed us. The only job my parents could get was dealing drugs. There were times we didn't see them for weeks. I would take care of my siblings, it felt natural to. I made sure they ate, went to school, and showered. My little sister still blames me for not potty training her sooner than the age of four, even though I am only six years older than her.

Because my parents were drug dealers, they brought the shadiest of people to our house (drug dealers, drug users, pimps and hookers). I had to watch whoever came through our door. I had to know if they were going to be a problem before they actually were, so that I could protect my siblings and keep them safe from the things I'd already experienced.

Physical disabilities hit me hard. At about twelve years old, I was at the state library. I turned to grab a magazine and all of a sudden I experienced a sharp pain from my lower back that shot all the way down to my toes. There were times I'd be out of school or work due to the pain. When the doctors would ask me to scale my pain from 1 to 10, I'd say 20 because it hurt that much. When I am in that state, the best thing to do is to leave me alone. There were times I wanted to chop my leg off and kill myself with it just to stop the pain. I could barely walk two feet in front of me without dropping to the ground.

Depression was a hard one to fight. My sister helped me to live for others until I could live for myself. I attempted suicide several times but somehow here I am still. I know God has a plan for me. The thing about depression is I have a good sense for detecting my "self" in others and always wish to help those in need. I don't know why. I have always been that way. Reflex?

The good things I've experienced are love, kindness, respect, compassion, self-sacrifice and self-awareness. These are all things we should share. When someone shows you these things you can't help but share them. Respect? Everyone starts out with my respect. It is up to the person, whether or not that changes. Self-sacrifice? The first one to teach me that was Jesus. My sister Ana is the second, because if she did not step in when my parents were imprisoned, we would all be separated and taken by CPS. I would probably never see them again. I am ever grateful to her.

My family was once very strong. We would cling to each other because no one would let their children play with us and it was very hard to trust anyone. This was a good thing because I love my family very much. A few disagreements between family members have left us all feeling abandoned. This is when I learned no one likes when someone tells them where they are wrong. And what forgiveness really means.

My boyfriend is very supportive and sweet. My mother went through physical, mental and emotional abuse. Her ex-husband knocked half her teeth out, broke a few of her ribs, and raped her in front of my siblings. An abusive guy would not get along with me. My boyfriend is not perfect, but all the qualities you hope your daughter would find in a man, I have in him.

Work has been very stressful. The things I've had to deal with while working security have been insane. Working at the library, I've had to deal with drug dealers, domestics, scary and shady characters, etc...I had to work with HPD on a regular basis. The stress was not worth the pay.

Family and friends encouraged me to pursue the law field I had been thinking of for some time now. I always figured law is a useful tool that won't break my back and is something I could do for the rest of my life.

While searching to see if Heald College had any classes in law, I left my information in hopes that I would get a packet in the mail or something. I received a call asking to meet. I wanted to show how serious I was about going to school again. It turned out that was the day I enrolled. I was sent to the financial advisor to see if I could get help paying for me to go to school, and once I saw that it was possible, I jumped at the chance.

When I had back pain and called in sick to work, they wanted a doctor's note. When I was finally able to bring in the note, which cost me 20 dollars, I resigned. They would not work with me going to school, even though I had given the company a good name and was helpful at every site. But my coworkers all missed me and I will keep them in my heart forever!

It seems like it was meant to be, like this is where God wanted me to be, considering how things unfolded and how fast it all happened. I've learned that there is no time like the present and sometimes you just have to drop yourself in it and work your way out.

Coming to Heald has made such a difference in my life already. Growing up the way we did? Set apart from others? It can really put you in a box. Now, having to get out of the box to work with others has proven to be a blessing. My teachers and classmates will be in my heart with all the rest of those I love. And one day, maybe we will see each other again.

Thank you, Ms. Sabrina! Your patience, understanding ways and teaching of visual strategies have shown me that finding what works best for me is beneficial to my success. My steady habits of procrastination and our planner assignments have shown me how often I really do procrastinate, how I don't say nice things to myself enough, and how filling out a planner ahead of time can actually help me plan all of these things and give me a monthly visual of my plans, commitments, activities, and even when to say something positive of myself or of the day.

When I think about living in the "Now" and preparing for the "Future," I hope that in five years, I will be making at least 24 to 28 dollars an hour as a paralegal. I'll probably be back in school because my goal is to be an attorney. I would also like to help my family in any way I can to better themselves. In ten years, I hope to be a lawyer, own a house, have a family and my own practice. Dreams are free!

I can do anything I put my mind to. I can pass the tests and do the work, on time. I am confident in taking the next steps ahead of me with Heald at my side, and with teachers like Ms. Sabrina, helping me to see who I am and who I can become.

Sabrina Favors (Ed)

Merging Two Halves:
From the Past to the Future

"You can never go home again, but the truth is
you can never leave home,
so it's all right."

- Maya Angelou

Transition

Adult storyteller from Paata, Chuuk

In Paata, Chuuk, I walk around my island with my kids, but here, it is different from my island because we catch the bus. Only the center of Chuuk has a bus where the plane lands, where we have big stores where the ships come in. On Fefan, the air force came to our place and fixed the roads where we also use cars, but they went back recently and the road isn't so good, because of the water coming in. There used to be plenty of people, and beautiful things in the store, but in Chuuk that isn't the case anymore.

For light, we used flashlights, and coconut leaves tied together that we burned. If I stay on my island I feel good, but here I don't feel good. When I am in Paata, I feel good because I sleep well, and whatever I want to do, I do. There I never think of paying rent and paying electric bills. When I am back home, I don't feel hurt because I didn't have to do other things with money, other things with the police, other things like go to appointments.

Back home, when we feel sick, we go to see the doctor, and if we have money, we pay for our medicine. But if we don't have money, they can just give us the medicine. When we are here, only the people who have medical insurance can see a doctor. So when we are sick, sometimes we cannot go see a doctor because we are scared. If we don't know how to speak English, we are worried about going; if we don't have medical insurance, we don't go.

Back home, we don't have to spend money for everything we need, only some things, like rice, chicken or canned meat, soap, and kerosene (for the lamp and stove). But here, we spend money for everything.

Even though I don't sleep at night here because I worry, I am also happy because of the changes, because of the modern things, and because my kids are in school. I am hoping that maybe I can be a part of it, I can change for the better so we look good and feel good. I think I need to blend in, but I didn't realize before that there are so many hard things to do before I can be like other Americans. To get to that goal, I have to get through many challenges.

But in Hawai'i, the beaches are nice. Where people go, they are clean, and that gives me happiness to see.

The Life of the Youngsters

Youth storyteller from Chuuk

A boy moves into Mayor Wright Housing, his name is T-Boy, from Micronesia.

He meets some bad boys who would pick on him. They took his things.

The bad boys live in Mayor Wright, too; they were neighbors. But one day, one of the bad boys came in and stood up for T-Boy, and TB and the bad boy, Kevin, became friends.

The moral of the story is how T-Boy changed Mayor Wrights. The bad boys stole cars and toy airplanes, and robbed stores, but TB taught them about the bible, and they started a basketball team at their church.

When TB went to Central Middle School that first day, he saw how bad everything was, and how everyone had a bad attitude towards the teachers, and there was graffiti everywhere. He tried to fit in and hang out with people. They would steal cars too, but he changed everyone. He watches NBA games and keeps things cool in the neighborhood.

a sad story: the dreams of the past

Youth storyteller from Chuuk

One guy came from Chuuk and he moved into a new place in the islands called Hawai'i. When he went to school, he met a friend. After a few months, they became best friends.

He had moved to Hawai'i for school, but had a hard time because he didn't know English and he didn't know any people. He got into fights. People would tease him, and he would knock them out, and then they left him alone, they didn't bother him anymore. T-Boy liked living in Hawai'i, it was better than Chuuk because school was better. And his family was a good family; they went to church every Sunday, and they liked living in Hawai'i, too, because they had better jobs.

They would talk about Chuuk, though, and how they want to go home and visit the people, because they missed them. Some people in Hawai'i were nice, but some were mean to the Chuukese, the odds of meeting one or the other were maybe 50-50. School was better since it had more supplies, and the education was an improvement. It was peaceful in Hawai'i, but T-Boy still dreamed—and planned—to build a castle back home, where he and his friends could always go.

Although T-Boy requested that we "add in wow words that look smart, but people understand," we felt none were needed.

Moving for Medical

Adult storyteller from Fefan

I've been living in Hawai'i since 2001. Ignacia is my niece. I moved here because hospitals transferred my daughter to Hawai'i.

My daughter and I arrived here first, and later, because I have nine children—I have six girls and three boys—my other children came. My oldest boy is still in Chuuk, but all of the rest of us are here. And I want to go back to Fefan because of my garden; I like to clean and cook in my home. When I was on the island, I did not have to work, my husband did, and I took care of the house. But when I came here with my daughter, she was seven years old, and I had to take care of her. But she died in 2009. She was fifteen years old. So I returned to Chuuk with my daughter and my family to take her body back home. I don't know how long I stayed with her, but I have children in school, so I had to come back. And I had to return for work, too. I did housekeeping for a family from Italy; they are rich and they live on Punchbowl. I liked the job, but it was fifteen-hour days. I would wait until they finished dinner, and clean everything up. I was there from morning to dinner, every day. A Filipina also worked from them. The other woman was like me, but in 2010, I was finished because my leg hurt a lot, and my daughter had to take over my job up to now.

Me, you know, I joined the program first to work, and it is good here because I have food and clothes, but it is very hard because if I cannot work, I don't have any money and I have to move out of my house.

It is good in Chuuk, because I can stay at home. We had it good there. My son is still there with my husband; he is not working because he has diabetes, and he had a stroke.

My daughter, Kercy, had a brain tumor, but she was very strong when she was born. She was very happy when we stayed in the house and watched a movie. She would remember some things, like songs. She loved Selena, and lots of the Disney movies—she would clap and cry. She would get so excited, and when her sister would come back from school and she would hear her footsteps, she would be very happy. She could talk but towards the end, Kercy couldn't talk anymore.

Here and now, for work and school, that is why my other kids live here. I have two girls and one boy working and the youngest one is still in school, tenth grade. I think, when I am tired, that I might go back home, but I am staying with my youngest daughter for two more years until she graduates. It is difficult to be here thinking about money for paying rent, paying off a car. But it is the best thing for my children. I have grandchildren, too; I have seven grandchildren. That is why it is best to be here. My oldest sister is on the Big Island (BI). I go and visit, and I like it better than here: fewer people, very quiet, more like Chuuk.

Kids and grandkids, I think they are getting a solid education here, but I often think about my youngest daughter, who wants to go to the mainland to stay in Wisconsin or Oregon. She wants to go now because her cousin says it is good, but she is not old enough. I tell her, "If you graduate from 12th grade, after that you can go."

Beyond Resilience

"Without work all life goes rotten,
But when work is soulless, life stifles and dies."

- Albert Camus

Keep on Keeping On

Adult storyteller from Chuuk, Fefan

I have been in Hawai'i more than ten years, and I came here to continue my education. I had a scholarship and financial aid from the US, but it didn't cover all the cost so I only went one year to HPU, but stopped going after that, because I had to work. I moved in with my friends and got a job at Zippy's. It was a good job, and I got a free lunch. That was in Kaneohe, and then I moved to Kalihi side, and I started working on a cruise ship. I found the job through a friend and it was fun; I would start at three in the afternoon and the boat would go out and then the cruise would be done by ten at night. Sometimes we would go whale-watching in the morning. It was fun working on the boat because I was used to working on boats. In Chuuk, the central island (Weno) has all the stores and government offices, so to get there from the outer island you have to go by boat. Fefan is so close to Weno, if it is calm, it takes half an hour; if it's rough, it is almost one hour. If you work on Weno, you commute into work every day from the other islands. The boats aren't crowded, because everyone has their own, just like in Hawai'i, where everyone has their own car. The boats are usually about eighteen feet long, and each family has one. So I am really used to boats.

After working for a few years, I tried to go back to school full time, maybe three or five years after I stopped. I had a full time job and was a full time student, but I was out late with my friends, too. It was hard. I finished the first semester, but I dropped out in the second. I worked at Safeway, the one on Beretania, part time, thirty hours a week. They had good benefits, medical and union membership. After that I worked for Handivan, I would drive the vans, so I resigned from Safeway because Handivan was full time. I found the job from my friend. I got my driver's license one week and the next week, I got hired. One time I was driving on H-3, coming down a hill, and my rear tire blew, so I slowly pulled over. The person that was with me said, "Oh, you are a good driver!" I called my office and a guy came with a tire and power tools and changed the tire and then I delivered my patient. We would help patients door to door, and if they were in wheelchairs, we would pull them up steps, everything.

I had met my wife in Guam and then we met again in Hawai'i. We got married while I worked as the Handivan driver. We got married at the HCC cafeteria in 2001. It was great. We have four kids, two boys, two girls. They are in tenth grade, ninth, sixth, and fifth.

I am glad we are in Hawai'i. My children have more opportunities to be whatever they want to be. It's the American dream. They are US citizens.

My last job was at HFM; it was at a warehouse. After I finished that job, it has been harder to find a good job. It's been almost a year, so I am going back to school. There are jobs now, but the pay is so low, and if I apply for the one with the higher pay, they require a college degree. My kids are getting older so I think I can go back to school. With a degree, I can get a better job here. If I go back to Chuuk, I know I will have a good job. Among my siblings—there are ten of us—I was the only one that reached college, so I will try my best.

My dad and two siblings are in Fefan, and they fish, maybe farm. One of my sisters lives in Guam. In Hawai'i, on Oahu, four of us live; my older brother drives a trailer and the other one, the youngest one, was going to go to school and now he works with his friend doing construction. Two live on the mainland, my sister is in Oregon, and then my other brother is in Kansas City. We have a good community over there, and if somebody moves to a place, some people talk and the others move. There are plenty of jobs, plenty of work; some work on the farm or in the meat packing industry, for Tyson. I thought about living there before, but not anymore. My other two brothers moved there and after two years they came back. They missed the islands. It feels kind of the same in Hawai'i as it does in Chuuk, and it is closer than on the mainland. When I first came, not too many Chuukese were here, now there are so many, they move from Guam and Chuuk and some move to the mainland and then they come back to Hawai'i.

Moving affects the young ones, most of them only speak English. They understand Chuukese, but it is hard for them to speak. More people are coming, but mostly they move to the mainland or BI (Big Island) because they heard about Oahu, people here know Chuukese, and people really discriminate. And not only that, but on the street, there are still fights between the Chuukese and the Samoans. It used to be worse, when I first moved here there were gangs who didn't really know Chuukese, we were so small and tight, we stuck together, but now there are many of us so people know us more. I don't have trouble with people if they don't know I am Chuukese, there are no problems. But if I tell them, or someone else tells them, then yes, people can be judgmental and mean.

No Place to Rest

Boys' Collaborative Poem
Youth poets from Chuuk and Tonga

Schoolwork
Schoolwork, math, so difficult.
I need help, now!
Free help now is the best.
It is the best answer, to making me pass.

Garden
It is beautiful, green, with so many colors.
Airy, and smelly.
Learned about aquaponics, and how to grow food
Bok choy, basil, lettuce, tomatoes.

Dreams
I want to become what I want to become
To be a regular person
Improving my technology skills for the future
I am the future, dreams.
Scary, to reach career goals

Become a man,
On your own
Choose your path.

Music
I am a rapper, I am a king,
Singing? I like to sing!
Play instruments, write songs
Sing together, harmonize
Create a band, let our voices be heard.

Family
Feel safe, happy, strong.
Close to each other, caring, loving
Wonderful.
I rely on them,
Always there.
Always been there.

Better life
Don't do drugs,
Do good things,
Get a better job,
Go to church, go to college, think about your future.
Think about your future.
Know about your future.
Help each other get there, and improve on your own skills.
Take care of yourself, be healthy.

Missing home

My roots are gone

Lost

Homeless, eating off the street

Dirty world

No job, no money.

No place to rest.

Turtle

I Keep Going

Adult storyteller from Fefan

I came in 2009 to Hawai'i for my kids that were staying here. I was thinking that I wanted to stay here and look for a job, make money, but since that time, I haven't gotten a job. I applied for many places, like Taco Bell, McDonalds, and some other restaurants. I live in Wahiawa and saw an opening over in Kaneohe and I applied, even though it was far. I applied to help myself and because I wanted to help my family. One job I did part time was bell-ringing before Christmas; they would drop us where they wanted us to go. Two years, maybe between 2010 and 2013, I would be in Wahiawa, where they would pick me up and take me places.

I am old so it is hard to stand for eight hours, but I try my best to do that. Everywhere I work, I work hard, and I am happy to have a job. My experience is in cooking in the kitchen; I clean, I don't mess around, all my bosses I work with really like me. Some of my bosses give me gifts, because they like me. In Guam on my birthday, one of my bosses gave me a gold ring that was my present from the family. When I worked on the golf course, security always gave me lunch; and at my other job, working in the fish market, my boss there took me to a nice restaurant for my birthday.

I am thinking, if these other people hire me and see how I work, how I do my job, how I clean, they would know. I had a place in Chuuk where they really wanted me to work, then I worked in Guam, also in the kitchen. One lady from Palau fired so many people, but she wanted me to stay. When I was on Guam, I worked at Taco Bell, 7-11, The Reef Hotel, and I drove, but one time I almost crashed so I quit that job. Afterwards, I only worked at Taco Bell and The Reef Hotel. My chief in the hotel asked me if I could quit my other job and work from nine to nine, but after that supervisor left, some of the workers complained about how I worked so many hours, so my second boss cut my hours. At that time, I worked part-time at a security job during the day, and I had to wait for someone to relieve me. I had a hard time getting to work on time at The Reef Hotel, so that is the one time I was fired. I went back to Fefan because my father was sick and I stayed with him until he died. After that, I came to Hawai'i to my kids, so I said okay, and I quit my other job, but because of the traffic on the road, I sometimes missed my other job. I was great at the hotel, I got a big salary there and worked twelve hours a day, working in the kitchen, cooking, and doing security.

When they terminated me, my manager asked what happened, and which one of the jobs, the hotel or the security, paid me more. When I said the hotel, he asked why I stayed at the other job. I just didn't say anything, but I like plenty of work. That is why I did it.

Then I knew that I would have time to work at a night shift, so my cousin, who worked at the golf course, told me to apply there. I would work at the golf course from ten to two in the morning. She liked the golf course, but was tired. I would walk around watching the place, to make sure nothing happened when they had people coming. It was scary. My cousin told me that people came to this place and saw ghosts and half people. One of my co-workers said when he put the radio in the security house, he came back and the radio was in the tree. There's even one room on the golf course that they don't go inside because when people stay there something else gets in the bed. I told them not to tell me about those stories. I worked on the weekends and I was happy.

When I stayed with my sister in Guam, the landlord had a catering business and they got me to work for them, then I would walk to work, and my bosses liked me; that is why I want to work. I enjoy my money to do whatever I want, I can shop, and share with my people that need help.

I still want to work, but maybe it is hard to hire people. Also I am thinking my age is a problem; I am older than others who apply, they know that. But why don't they just hire me and see how I work? This time around, I came here to help my auntie—we really have to help, especially my mom and my dad, her sister and her brother. I saw my auntie here moving around, and I didn't want to stay and *not* work, and I *want* to work, too. I work so hard, and want to finish my job.

I feel good about when I apply for jobs, but don't when I don't get hired. In the meantime, I volunteer at Wahiawa Elementary School. One time, something happened at the school my grandkids attend, and they gave us food. They just gave.

I can still do the job, maybe better than some people that go in and out of jobs. I keep going.

Hope is Alive

Debra Puailoa

I had a hard life growing up. When I was two years old I was raped, teased and put down by my stepdad and mother. My mom let my stepdad do those bad things to me. She was scared of my stepdad because he was very scary and crazy. He would stalk me everywhere I went. My own mother called me a whore and that hurt me the most. I didn't have any friends that I could run to for help. Sometimes I felt like ending my life and I felt dirty. I was the only girl and the oldest of three children. I was also raped by a relative. I remember yelling for help, but nobody would come. It went on a long time until I was eighteen. I finally said I need to get help so I went to my teacher. The first thing we did was call the police and they arrested my stepdad for raping a minor. He stayed in jail for five years and then went to the mental hospital for another five years. I never saw him again. After he came out of the mental hospital, he passed away. I still have memories, but I've forgiven him. He was still my father. My mom was my real mom; I forgave her a long time ago. She passed away three years ago at the age of 75. I miss her so much.

Now, I have moved on with my life. I have two beautiful children and am now a college student. I am also a single mom and it is great!

My kids are very happy. I have one boy, Daniel, and one girl, Soana, and they are my life. Today, I can say I am a survivor of domestic and sexual abuse.

In five years, I hope to be an RN (registered nurse) and to have a home for me and my kids. Hopefully, I will be making more money. I hope that my daughter goes to college, too, and that she goes to Heald.

Education:

Pathways to Opportunities and Change

"Them that's got shall get, Them that's not shall lose. So the Bible says, And it still is news. Mama may have, Papa may have, But God bless the child that's got his own."

- Billie Holiday, Arthur Herzog, Jr., "God Bless the Child"

Two Brothers

Adult storytellers from Chuuk

Once upon a time, there were two brothers Rongosich, the younger brother, and Rongonaa, the older brother. When anyone asked Rongonaa to do something, he wouldn't listen, but Rongosich always listened to his father when he asked him something. Rongonaa wouldn't listen to his father because he knew that as the oldest, he could do what he wanted.

The oldest child in a family is revered too much maybe, has too much freedom.

For his whole life, Rongosich, as the youngest, did all the work, farming, fishing, everything in the house. Rongosich thought it was his responsibility. When their dad asked Rongosich to do something, like "Rongosich, go to the farm and bring us some banana or potato," he would go and bring, but when the dad asked, "Rongonaa, go to the farm and find something to eat," the elder brother would say, "Ask Rongosich to do something for us, I am too important." And Rongosich would always listen and do it even if he was tired, even at night, even if they would ask all the time. He would do it.

The chief heard about the brothers. He wanted to see for himself, so he sent for the brothers to come to him. The chief was very old, and when the brothers came, they started to talk, and the chief stopped them. He wanted to ask them to do something for him, so he asked Rongosich to go to the mountain and bring a coconut for him, and he asked Rongonaa to go to the water and bring one fish. So they went, and maybe after three hours, Rongosich came back with the coconut and Rongonaa left and didn't come back. He didn't know how to catch the fish, so instead, he went home. The chief realized Rongonaa was not coming back, so he told Rongosich, "You go home and you tell your brother that tomorrow you have to come back and see me again."

Rongosich went home and the next day he brought his brother back to see the chief and the chief said, "Rongonaa, when I asked you to go to the water and bring me fish, you didn't listen and when I asked Rongosich to go to the mountain and bring me the coconut, he brought it to me, he listened to me, so from now on Rongosich will be the chief because he listens to me when I ask him."

Then Rongosich became the chief of the village, even though he was the youngest in the village. Even though Rongonaa was supposed to be the chief, because he didn't listen, he didn't become chief, and his younger brother did.

I Am Looking Forward

Tony Gilbert, from St. Louis, Missouri

There is so much to tell, but to give you a shortened version, I am an Air Force brat. I have three siblings, two brothers and a younger sister. I moved all over the place so diversity has always been out there; sometimes we were the only black family, like when we lived in Iceland. Things were good in my childhood, until I lost my mother when I was fourteen. We were in Illinois, Scott Air Force Base. So you know, that really changed things. That is when everything changed. Life just went somewhere else. I didn't even know what was going on, I didn't know what was happening. She was the glue that held it all together.

Needless to say, I went through a fog, probably for the next four years after my mother died. I didn't go to school all the time, and thought, "Who cares about grades?" Then, in my senior year, I almost didn't graduate, and it wasn't because of grades, but because of my attendance. You have to attend a certain number of days. So basically, the principle called me into his office and said I needed to finish it out, and not miss a day, so I did, because I didn't want my dad kicking my butt. I graduated.

After that, I went to work for two years; I partied and played. Then I decided to go into the army in 1984. I had a good career for three years, but I got tired of people telling me what to do, so I thought, "Hum, I'm gonna get out and become an officer and then go back in and tell other people what to do." But things didn't work out that way. There was cocaine out there, so I did a little and got distracted, for quite a few years. People say that doesn't happen to people who have good families, or have these types of privileges and everything like that, but they're wrong because I did have that, but drugs don't care. Basically, I ended up being out there, got arrested, and my family was not too happy about that, but they still supported me. They have always supported me, regardless.

I ended up in California, in San Francisco, and things were really rough, 'cause I just wasn't ready to accept that alcohol and drugs had a hold on me. I kept saying, "I can handle it," but that just was not true. Around 2000, I said okay, I had enough, there has got to be something else to it. I went to a Veterans Affairs hospital in White City, Oregon, and I basically started to, you know, digest what was really going on with me, and realized that a lot of people were going through the same thing. I learned that if you educate yourself, you can do better. You don't need to get arrested.

I stayed in White City for fourteen years. I didn't think much about college, but the VA would pay for it, so I said okay, I want to be doing something, and I took an English class and a math class, just to be taking them. I was kind of bored. I said, "I am not good, it has been a while." I went to work then, and just did the whole normal thing.

My brother lives in Hawai'i, and he kept bugging me. "Come on, man, come to Hawai'i." Finally, I said, "Okay, here I come."

I got off the plane, and was just getting used to the islands when he told me, "You have to go to school." I said, "Uhhh no. Nooo! Leave me alone." He was like, "You've got Chapter 33, they're paying for everything, and they give you a salary." I said, "They give you extra money, extra money to go to school?" He said "Yeah!" So I said, "Okay." He had a friend that worked in the office at Heald, and I came in to talk, but before I left, they pretty much had me already signed up.

After not being in school for a while, being back in classes, you know, brother was not happy. In the first term, one of the classes, COMP 103, was just computers. And I am going, "Wait, all these tools." I wasn't happy about it, but I had to deal with it myself. It has been a difficult transition. Excel and Outlook are hard. I know how to type emails, and send them, but these other programs were complicated. One of the things about me is, when I am under pressure, I shut down. But, in this class, instead of getting mad, I got a tutor to help me. My brother knows everything about computers, inside and out. He was able to help me; he explained it to me and broke it down. He showed me things, and then had me do them with him there.

I wanted to get a degree in business administration with an emphasis on hospitality and tourism. I figured this is a good place to do it, work for a cruise liner, start as an activities coordinator, and then take over as the director. So yeah, that is where I am at right now. I am finishing these two classes, COMP 103 and Success 100. I feel good about passing Success 100. The teacher, Sabrina Favors, wow, she is great. She really is. But I am looking forward to the next quarter. I have math, writing, and keyboarding. I like those classes.

My brother really pushes me. He is also back in school, getting his masters. To keep it real, he keeps going because he likes money. In his field, you can only get so high until you hit a pay ceiling, so he is back in school; he is hungry for it. And that is what he is helping me with, to keep pushing. I was happy making 20,000 to 30,000 dollars a year, I was comfortable. But there are things I want to do, like travel. I love to travel, so I need money. I have traveled to Germany three times, but I don't think I would go back to Iceland again, way up there.

I have had lots of experiences and after a good twelve years, I am back in school. Some of the classes I took are frustrating, but the atmosphere has changed for the better since coming here. In White City, the diversity is not so great. There are blacks because of the VA facility, but not like here. Being here, I was able to take a deep breath and go, "All right, everybody isn't looking at you like you're crazy," you know. Asking myself, "What are you doing over here?" that is a really nice change.

In My Dreams

Youth storyteller from Aiea, Hawai'i

I work really hard in school because my dad is a teacher and he pushes me. I like to go to Na Hokulele because I can do my homework, and receive help with it. If I don't come here, sometimes it is hard to do work after school.

In my dreams

In my dreams, I dream about going to college.
When I am in college, I go by the rules, and get good grades,
I play basketball and win a lot of awards.
I become a police officer.

In my life now, I babysit my sister's children,
I always go to practice basketball,
And I like to come here, and do my homework.

Voice and Empowerment

"Education should not be the filling of a pail, but the lighting of a fire."
- William Butler Yeats

"…Youth voice is crucial to the overall effectiveness of service-learning programs. Youth voice has a tremendous impact on program participation and program outcomes, both short term and long term."
- Education Commission of the States

Letters From Students at St. Damien Memorial School

NHP included an in-class project with sophomores at St. Damien Memorial School in Honolulu. These tenth graders learned about and voiced their opinions on authentic issues in their communities, wrote letters to their legislators and created artwork that was shown at the Honolulu Museum of Art. They actively engaged in decision-making and showed that students can impact the future of where they live. Included are excerpts from their letters to legislators.

Student Letter-Writers:

Christien Ayson

William Bagley

Melany Batad

Ian Bento

Skyler Capllonch

Christian Cubacub

Tuiletuli Fua

Graham Gibson

Justen Herodies

Jacob Isler

Carina Iwane

Kennedy Kauwenaole

Josiah Ladiero

Mikayla Min

Brooke Moreilhon

Rhiannon Palmere

Kelsey'Joy Perreira

Jayvee Reuben Quines

Christian Uemura

I am a student at Damien Memorial School and I have been talking to my classmates about improving construction on Hickam Air Force Base. People are beginning to get irritated with all the construction work that is going on because it is closing down important roads and taking away from the beauty of the community... People have things they like to see while walking or driving by. All of this construction is either taking down or blocking the beauty of the community.

I am a teenager who lives in Pauoa and would like to address an issue that can be prevented. I've witnessed many cars speeding up and down my road, ignoring stop signs. It is dangerous for kids to walk to school because they might get hit by a car. It is also dangerous for the elderly who take walks throughout the day, or people exercising or walking their dogs. This issue does not only happen in Pauoa, but in many communities on the island. I think more people would travel to their destination by foot if they felt safer on the roads. I believe a major accident can be prevented by posting more speed limit signs... Another way is by posting signs that say watch for pedestrians or children at play.

In my neighborhood, the roads and sidewalks are very narrow. There is limited space to play outside on the sidewalk, and when I see that a car is coming down the street, it is very close to the sidewalk. There should be more speed limit signs. There were multiple times that two cars were coming in opposite directions, and one car was speeding down and almost hit another car. There should be more room on the sidewalks and more speed limit signs so pedestrians and cars don't get hurt.

Some of our roads have recently been improved, but there are still many roads that can be hazardous to the safety of a driver. The potholes on the roads, for instance, can be very dangerous. Often, they are left for quite some time and finally, after countless cars have gone over them, possibly scraping their cars, the potholes are fixed. We can fix these hazardous road problems by being more aware, and citizens can report the location, and so the problem of fixing it can become faster. Another thing is the size of the sidewalks…We can fix the sidewalks so that we can keep our citizens safe.

I believe that [the rail] will not benefit my neighborhood nor my school's neighborhood in any significant way. Although the rail project has not begun construction in the areas I commute to, I experience traffic and road closures along the way due to the drilling of soil for foundation samples…I also believe this project will cause clutter in the neighborhood, and the modernized style would take away from the beauty and simplicity of the neighborhoods.

As high school students, we spend a gigantic part of our time going to and from school, social events, and after-school activities.

Most of us do not drive...I find myself leaving home at an earlier time only to arrive at school at a later time than previously. To solve the traffic problems, the state government has pushed the idea of an island rail system, which I find to be a step in the wrong direction that will not solve the problems of traffic and congestion. Those in favor of rail have failed to keep in mind cost and funding problems...Instead, I propose the state should look toward investing into road repairs and expansion. By building and improving our roads, we can alleviate some of the problems we face at a lower cost when compared to rail.

An issue I'd like to warn you about is the construction and completion of the rail system. The rail will close roads down and will create more traffic throughout our beautiful island. Next, the rail will not only create havoc, but will be a step backwards in our society. The rail system just shows how much of the island we can use up before it turns into a wasteland.

I believe we should not have the rail system for many reasons. One, it will alter the exquisite scenery of Hawai'i. The rail system might obscure the nature that is Hawai'i. Also, it will take a lot of time to complete, which can cause traffic problems while the rail system is being built. Lastly, trash might get thrown under the rail system, which can cause major pollution that will degrade the beauty of Hawai'i.

Many of my friends complain about the financial burden the rail project might have on their families. They are worried that the rail project would require increased taxes to offset the cost. In addition, another concern is that, while the rail project is under construction, transportation would be more difficult and time-consuming due to closed-off roads.

I am aware that when the rail is built, there will be several rail stations available to pedestrians wanting to ride the rail transit. However, there are several problems that arise with this, one of them is increased traffic. Given that there will be a significant number of people riding rail, there will likely be an increase of pedestrians and commuters trying to get to the rail stations. So possibly, new roads could be built in an effort to diffuse this influx of traffic.

Traffic situations seem to be one of the root causes for this rail project. And yes, I agree, traffic here is crazy. But I do not think that building a rail will help out the situation in any way. Raising taxes and taking away from the natural beauty of this island by putting a giant obstructing rail transit on it does not seem worth it. Face it, people like taking their own cars. It is less of a hassle than waiting for a bus or a rail to come and pick you up, and you can throw everything in your car that you need for the day. It is basically just more of a convenience.

The problem that will arise when the rail is built, is that traffic will not decrease, but will only be moved. What you and the entire community can do to help solve this problem, is to make drivers more aware of pedestrians as they travel to the rail stations. Although I dislike the idea of the rail project, I should at least care and support those who want it and will be traveling on the rail.

Having a rail system will truly benefit the transportation infrastructure as a whole. The rail system will provide a fast alternative to driving. Fewer drivers mean that we can alleviate some of the traffic problems occurring on our highways. Three stations in the neighborhood are going to be really convenient for us; however, this benefit introduces some problems. One of them is traffic. In the Kalihi/Palama area, roads are already packed during rush hour. How will the roads be able to handle the cars traveling to stations? Pedestrian sidewalks and crosswalks will also gain traffic due to people accessing the stations by foot. The large amounts of vehicles and pedestrians will cause a bottleneck, slowing the transportation efficiency of this neighborhood even more. Yet, as young students who are not able to drive, our main options are walking and the bus system. The rail project is really important to the current and future youth of the island.

I want to make sure that we [students] have a voice in the issue of this rail becoming a huge factor in our area. Although I am pro rail, there are issues I have questions about. The most important issue for our neighborhood moving forward is the issue of traffic and if this will be a viable resource for citizens. I commute to my school every day by car and there is always traffic. Will this rail reduce traffic for all people who commute to the East side daily? Or will it cause traffic to be more severe...I'd also like to be assured if this rail would actually be put to use. There is a lot of money going into the cost and funding to develop the rail.

Because of traffic and the incapability of getting to certain areas in a fast enough time, I would like to say a rail system would benefit many people. Helping citizens like myself by building this rail system would be of much help.

I need to wake up at 5:00 a.m. and must leave my house at 5:30 a.m. to be able to arrive at school on time, around 7:00 to 7:20 a.m. However, my classmates and I have found a solution to this issue. Extend the rail further west. This is a controversial topic and has a high possibility of not being put in action. Fortunately, another solution is at hand. The reason why a daily commute takes so long is because there are only two ways to get to that one area…Our solution is to create another route to the eastern part of Oahu.

I believe that the rail transit system will be for the betterment of Hawai'i. I think that the rail will have a positive outcome on Oahu and its traffic issues. Not only does Hawai'i have one of the worst traffic problems in the U.S., but we also have many accidents that occur daily…Rail will help ease the traffic by taking cars off the road and allowing people to save money on gas. Currently, many areas in neighborhoods lack space for people to walk, so having rail allows people to avoid these areas and get to their destination safely.

I am in support of rail because, for one, that would mean fewer cars on the road, so the traffic is spread out. Rail could hold and transport 400 passengers in two train-cars. This would improve traffic in the most over-populated parts of the island. The twenty-one stations from Kapolei to Ala Moana would provide a simpler and more efficient method of transportation. Also, rail could eliminate, or at least lessen, the number of pedestrian deaths.

As someone who is not legally able to drive myself yet, I, along with my classmates, often struggle to achieve the transportation we need to go to school, public services like libraries, school-sponsored elective and athletic events, and almost everywhere else we are required to be. Seeking public transportation, carpools, or even biking can be especially difficult for many in my class, as not everyone lives in convenient proximity to our school. One of my comrades is required to begin biking many miles to the closest bus stop at 4:30 a.m. every day in order to make it to school on time (7:40). For another, the commute home is even more strenuous, requiring a full two hours of bus jumping and walking, all while possessing school and sports supplies. There are hundreds of other examples of incredible and insane commutes required by these minors in order to get where they need to go. This is unsatisfactory, and I compel you to see that this is a statewide issue that must be solved by the bolstering of public transportation...[F]or myself, my comrades, and the thousands of others suffering, I urge you to use your power in this state to uphold this project and to help bring this great state closer to transportation equality.

A week after sending his letter, this last student received a response, excerpted below:

With regards to an expanded transportation system, any proposal inevitably comes to the question of cost. The City could expand TheBus, but passenger fares account for only a third of the total operating cost. That means federal funding and county revenues, derived from taxes, must make up the balance. I don't believe dramatically raising bus fares, or increasing taxes to pay for more service, would be appealing to riders or taxpayers...

As for roads, we don't have much room to expand our freeway system, and even if we did, construction would require billions of tax dollars and ongoing maintenance would only add to our long-term financial burden. So far, proposals to expand our freeway system have all involved building freeways on top of freeways. You can imagine the visual blight stacked freeways would create, as well as the years of traffic congestion during the construction phase.

I believe the rail system is our best hope for the near future. With rail comes what's called transit-oriented development. This is where residences and businesses (and maybe schools) are developed in the area surrounding the transit stations, thereby lessening commute times for many.

- Donna Mercado Kim, Hawai'i State Senate President

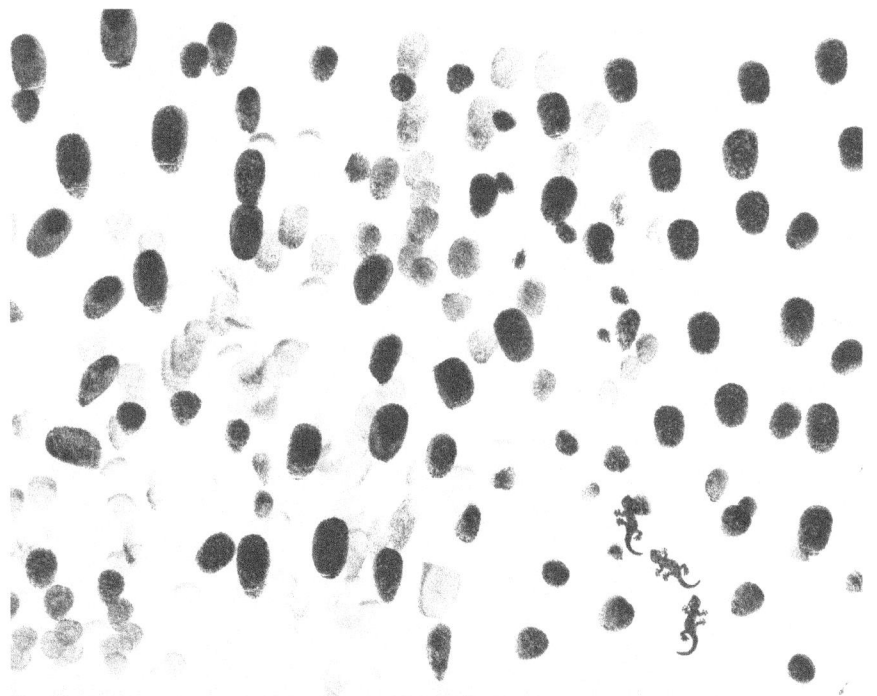

Fingerprints of Many

Commentary

Looking Back and Beyond

Father David Gierlach
Priest, St. Elizabeth's Episcopal Church

The Chuukese people are among the most respectful, kind and generous people to have ever found a home in our Hawaiian Islands. They come from what seem to be specks on the map in a distant corner of the vast Pacific Ocean. They come here because half a century ago, when the world went mad with thermonuclear bomb testing, it was this remote corner of the globe that was chosen to be ground zero. The people living on the beautiful green atolls, surrounded by aqua marine lagoons, were either pushed away from their ancestral lands, or, for those allowed to stay, saw subsistence economies based on fishing and farming and pandanus-roofed homes replaced by white rice, SPAM and corrugated metal huts. They migrate here seeking a decent education for their children and badly needed medical care for a population with an abundance of cancer, kidney failure and diabetes. They share everything they have, no matter how little they have. They are a faith-filled people who are happiest when they have fed strangers and friends alike. And when they arrive on these, our islands, they smile that ever-so-present shy smile and say to us: "Thank you for allowing us to live here." And I weep in the face of such gracious forgiveness.

The Importance of Culture

One challenge in an anthology such as this was, not only the language barrier, gathering stories from many for whom English is a second language, but from the cultural barriers hidden within language. When asked to "share their stories," some Chuukese participants recited tales, myths and legends that were told to them by older generations. It soon came to light that the Chuukese had different words for stories of mythical and legendary figures, and stories that recounted their own lives and experiences, which they considered more "news" than "story."

In some cases, the tales they told reflected immutable, familial values—the importance of hard work, listening to your family, sticking close to your children, and being careful what you wish for. These stories have been included in the main anthology. One contribution, however, didn't quite fit with the themes of the anthology. And yet, "The Tale of Crab and Rat" relates something important about the culture of many of the anthology contributors. Thus, it has been included in its own section, to highlight a compelling aspect of Chuukese culture and etiquette.

The Tale of Crab and Rat

Kathy Andereas

Once upon a time, there was a crude, young rat. He lived on the island of Paren, Chuuk. There was a *nipwei* (crab), and the crab also lived on the island. The crab and the rat talked to each other and decided to go to the other side of the island together. When they walked on the road on the other side of the island, they saw this *fach* (pandanus) tree full of ripe fruit. The rat asked the crab to climb the tree and get the fruit, but when the crab climbed the tree, he lost a leg. He climbed the tree again and lost another leg. He kept trying and losing legs until they were all gone. Then rat climbed the tree.

When the rat reached the top of the tree, he ate the *fach*, but did not throw any down for the crab. He ate until there was almost no more *fach* to give to the crab. There was only one more piece of fach, but the rat cleaned his armpits with it, and his backside, and then threw it down for the crab. But it smelled *ponou* (awful), so he couldn't eat it.

Finally, the rat went down to the crab and said, "Let's go home." The rat was very full and very happy, but not the crab.

Some time passed, and the crab forgave the rat, because you must forgive and you must share, and said, "I have something for you to eat. If you want it, you come and eat." But the rat said, "I don't want anything from you, Crab. I don't like your food."

The crab asked again, offering another food, and the rat, rude as he was, said, "I don't like that food."

Then the crab decided he'd had enough, and would make what the rat likes, so he made cobra. He set the food up with a noose around it to catch the rat, and then he asked the rat if he liked *taka* (coconut meat and cobra). The rat said yes. Then the crab told him that he could go eat. The rat ran over and began to hungrily claw at the food and he got caught in the trap. The rat called out to the crab, "Let me go!" But the crab said, "*Tup tup nakich, non ai chunimei, tere kik tere kik tere kik kik* (I caught you in a trap and you are a rat)."

The moral of the story is that you must share. It is similar to the saying "what goes around comes around," or "do unto other as you would do to yourself," but is not as much about one person, as it is about a community. In our culture, especially in our clan, we share everything. It is also rude to say no, or not accept when someone offers something to you. If you are not hungry, or if you do not like the food that is offered, you just pretend and eat some. Being like the rat is the worst thing someone can be.

Afterword: The Na Hokulele Project

Na Hokulele ("Shooting Stars"), a grant program funded by the Department of Housing and Urban Development, Office of University Partnerships, Alaska Native/Native Hawaiian Institutions Assisting Communities (AN/NHIAC) Program, continues to meet or exceed its goals in the Kalihi-Palama community. Below are brief snapshots highlighting NHP's initial years (2011 -2014).

I.   NHP Goals

Goal 1: Provide children with meaningful after-school care that focuses on overall development of the child.

Goal 2: Provide adults in the community with information that leads to increased literacy and community-economic-workforce development.

Goal 3: Meaningfully engage the community through workshops and community meetings.

II. Curriculum

Science Technology Engineering Math (STEM)

Students in NHP receive STEM related education and training through direct interaction and guidance from student mentors from

Hawai'i Pacific University, University of Hawai'i at Manoa and Chaminade University of Honolulu, as well as several local community colleges. Community partners, such as the Honolulu Museum of Art, also provide mentors for our participants. Field trips augmented what students learned in the afterschool STEM-focused classes. The STEM focus also includes a wide range of lessons including, but not limited to, marine science, kinesiology, health and nutrition, urban transportation and age friendly communities.

Literacy

The middle and high school students focused on vocabulary and comprehension in literature circles (or "read aloud sessions"). They read *Unwind* (a popular, futuristic, science fiction novel), and as students completed each chapter of the book, they discussed what they learned, often making comparisons to their own cultural context. For example, the boys from the island thought that the responsibility between males and females should not be shared; that each gender has its own set of roles and responsibilities. Many of the boys said that they believed that if a girl decides to have a child, it is her sole responsibility to care for the child, while it is the father's responsibility to provide food and shelter for the family. Conversely, the girls in the class disagreed, declaring that parenting should be a joint effort between mothers and fathers. The preschool through grade 5 participants focused primarily on word study (letter/sound relationships) in the context of comprehension of literature and texts. The younger children read picture books learning about colors and shapes, while making up their own stories. The older students read meaningful text and wrote stories focusing on self-awareness and self-image. Students learned to listen carefully, to observe, and to sound out words and identify letters and letter patterns. Nearly 90% of the students learned to recite and recognize all of the letters in the alphabet and correctly pronounce many new words. Additionally, most of the younger students learned to write all of the letters of the alphabet free hand (without tracing) in upper and lower case. All NHP literacy curriculum is aligned with State Common Core Standards.

Adult Job Readiness and Workforce Development

The adult job readiness and workforce development program at St. Elizabeth's Episcopal Church, or at other locations supporting job skills and internships such as the University of Hawai'i, Magoon Research and Teaching Facility (MRTF), in partnership with the St. Elizabeth's First to Work outreach, provides information to participants about Sustainable Agriculture and Personal Care Attendant training in addition to: (a) goal setting; (b) how to use computers and basic computer skills; (c) resume writing (e.g. cover letter, prior employment and volunteer experiences and skills); (d) general writing (e) basic job search; (f) interview preparation and (h) opportunities in education (high school, GED and college). To date, thirty-five adults enrolled in the Saturday program found employment and one participant enrolled in college.

Leadership Skills

Adults, youth and children learn leadership skills. To date 98% have successfully completed learning activities in critical thinking, innovation, problem solving, research, focus, time management, attitude, self-discipline, integrity, collaboration/networking, organization, and effective communication.

Digital Media

Children and youth (grades 4-12) with an interest in digital media and filmmaking integrated the job skills/leadership training values into personal stories about their lives and experiences. Under the mentorship of an experienced filmmaker, students' filming techniques improved over time and their willingness to share their thoughts and ideas through collaboration, strengthened. An important goal was to teach children and youth to develop their own voice through discussions about culture, responsibility and envisioning their future. Another goal was for students to learn about the film editing process. The film students produced two short films, each integrating contemporary music, dance and the concepts of community and culture. They included footage of their games (basketball and marbles); stories about the preparations of food (e.g., farming techniques and processing coconut); navigating new places (their neighborhoods); and achievements in their education (reading, science experiments and homework). Two screenings, to the delight of everyone, were held for both the young filmmakers and the local community residents.

A parallel project offered to adults involved filming the progress of a garden located at the university. Filming took place every Saturday and captured the transformation of the garden on a weekly basis. Initially, the adults were reluctant to be around the camera, but gradually most of them became comfortable and were willing to share their stories with one another about their gardens in Chuuk and their knowledge of herbs and medical uses for plants. This project culminated in the filming of the project participants' successful produce sale at the annual St. Elizabeth's church bazaar.

Field Trips

Children and adults participate in regular field trips, but perhaps the most important outings are the four trips a year to local public and university libraries. For many students, this is their first experience going to a library. The library tour includes visits to the different special collections (Hawaiian, Rare and Book Arts, and MAGIS (Maps, Aerials, and GIS), where students learn about the purpose that each collection serves. Students are especially intrigued by the MAGIS collection where spatial information is created and analyzed. The room includes numerous computers, large format printers and highly specialized remote sensing software. Students appreciate and benefit from the library staff's "show me how" approach, in which young visitors can first observe, and then try the same thing on their own afterwards.

III. Community Engagement

Information sessions are held regularly for parents and community members and include topics such as: Turning Problems to Success; Time Management and Success; Effort Pays Off; and Communication and Success. Turning Problems to Success addresses the common challenges that immigrants to Hawai'i often encounter, such as employment, housing and children's schooling. Various techniques to address and solve the problems are discussed and many audience members ask questions, share their personal situations and are given advice or referred to someone who might assist them. As a result, additional activities are developed and added to the curriculum (e.g., Urban Transportation, Age-Friendly Cities) to meet the needs of children, adults and community members. One-on-one sessions are also held with parents once a month to provide them with updates on their child's academic progress in NHP.

IV. Community Support

The brief examples of community support described below are representative of the abundant, collaborative assistance our community provides to NHP and for which we are truly grateful.

St. Elizabeth's Episcopal Church

NHP is situated on the campus of the St Elizabeth's Episcopal Church. Project staff soon recognized that children were arriving to the afterschool program from school hungry and needed a mid-afternoon snack. St. Elizabeth's, in addition to making space, utilities, a passenger van and parking available at no cost to the grant project provides mid-afternoon snacks and a hot, dinner meal to upwards of forty-five children (and sometimes their parents). Likewise, all program participants receive hot breakfast on Saturday mornings while enrolled in NHP. St. Elizabeth's also provides transportation services for up to twenty-one students who live too far to walk to and from the program site.

Barnes & Noble

A Na Hokulele Project book fair, sponsored by a local Barnes and Noble Booksellers Store was held in fall 2012. A total of 152 books were donated by our sponsor. Additionally, Barnes and Noble collected 1,809 books during the 2012 holiday season, which they gifted to NHP which was designated as one of their community partners. These opportunities support our community literacy efforts as the books received go directly into the homes of our participating families in the low-income community served by the project.

Times Coffee Shop in Kailua

The Times Coffee Shop, a local, family-owned diner, provided invaluable support to NHP by donating boxes of healthy food every week for the children's Friday "My Backpack Program." This project component allows each child attending the after-school program to take home a backpack filled with nutritious food to supplement the family's groceries over the weekend when healthy and nutritious meals may not be available.

Savant Books and Publications

Savant Books and Publications has assisted immensely in the creation of this anthology. SBAP has volunteered all editing and project supervision, and will be providing 150 complimentary soft cover books to NHP; book review copies as necessary; and 5% of net product sales donated to NHP to assist in project continuation.

About the Editor

Savant editor **Sabrina Favors** holds a Bachelor's degree in English and Psychology, and a Master's degree in English from the University of Hawai'i at Manoa. She has an eclectic taste in nonfiction, but with a preference for history, art, psychology, and folklore. She is also interested in fantasy of any sub-genre—from epic fantasy to urban, young adult and middle grade. Anything with a new twist or an unexpected take on an old tale

Visit her blog at http://redinkedleaf.blogspot.com/

If you enjoyed *Written in the Stars,* consider these other fine books from Savant Books and Publications:

Essay, Essay, Essay by Yasuo Kobachi
Aloha from Coffee Island by Walter Miyanari
Footprints, Smiles and Little White Lies by Daniel S. Janik
The Illustrated Middle Earth by Daniel S. Janik
Last and Final Harvest by Daniel S. Janik
A Whale's Tale by Daniel S. Janik
Tropic of California by R. Page Kaufman
Tropic of California (the companion music CD) by R. Page Kaufman
The Village Curtain by Tony Tame
Dare to Love in Oz by William Maltese
The Interzone by Tatsuyuki Kobayashi
Today I Am a Man by Larry Rodness
The Bahrain Conspiracy by Bentley Gates
Called Home by Gloria Schumann
Kanaka Blues by Mike Farris
First Breath edited by Z. M. Oliver
Poor Rich by Jean Blasiar
The Jumper Chronicles by W. C. Peever
William Maltese's Flicker by William Maltese
My Unborn Child by Orest Stocco
Last Song of the Whales by Four Arrows
Perilous Panacea by Ronald Klueh
Falling but Fulfilled by Zachary M. Oliver
Mythical Voyage by Robin Ymer
Hello, Norma Jean by Sue Dolleris
Richer by Jean Blasiar
Manifest Intent by Mike Farris
Charlie No Face by David B. Seaburn
Number One Bestseller by Brian Morley
My Two Wives and Three Husbands by S. Stanley Gordon
In Dire Straits by Jim Currie
Wretched Land by Mila Komarnisky
Chan Kim by Ilan Herman

Who's Killing All the Lawyers? by A. G. Hayes
Ammon's Horn by G. Amati
Wavelengths edited by Zachary M. Oliver
Almost Paradise by Laurie Hanan
Communion by Jean Blasiar and Jonathan Marcantoni
The Oil Man by Leon Puissegur
Random Views of Asia from the Mid-Pacific by William E. Sharp
The Isla Vista Crucible by Reilly Ridgell
Blood Money by Scott Mastro
In the Himalayan Nights by Anoop Chandola
On My Behalf by Helen Doan
Traveler's Rest by Jonathan Marcantoni
Keys in the River by Tendai Mwanaka
Chimney Bluffs by David B. Seaburn
The Loons by Sue Dolleris
Light Surfer by David Allan Williams
The Judas List by A. G. Hayes
Path of the Templar - Book 2 of The Jumper Chronicles by W. C. Peever
The Desperate Cycle by Tony Tame
Shutterbug by Buz Sawyer
Blessed are the Peacekeepers by Tom Donnelly and Mike Munger
The Bellwether Messages edited by D. S. Janik
The Turtle Dances by Daniel S. Janik
The Lazarus Conspiracies by Richard Rose
Purple Haze by George B. Hudson
Imminent Danger by A. G. Hayes
Lullaby Moon (CD) by Malia Elliott of Leon & Malia
Volutions edited by Suzanne Langford
In the Eyes of the Son by Hans Brinckmann
The Hanging of Dr. Hanson by Bentley Gates

Coming Soon:
Elaine of Corbenic by Tima Z. Newman
Flight of Destiny by Francis Powell
Ballerina Birdies by Marina Yamamoto
http://www.savantbooksandpublications.com

127

www.ingramcontent.com/pod-product-compliance
Lightning Source LLC
Chambersburg PA
CBHW060811250626
47162CB00005B/1741